The Translated Texts for Historians
COLOURING BOOK

Illustrated by Mark Humphries

Liverpool
University
Press

First published 2025 by

Liverpool University Press
4 Cambridge Street
Liverpool
L69 7ZU

Copyright © 2025 Mark Humphries

Mark Humphries has asserted the right to be identified as the author of this book in accordance with the Copyright, Designs and Patents Act 1988.

All rights reserved. No part of this book may be reproduced stored in a retrieval system, or transmitted, in any form or by any means, electronic, mechanical, photocopying, recording, or otherwise, without the prior written permission of the publisher.

British Library Cataloguing-in-Publication Data
A British Library CIP Record is available.

ISBN 978-1-83624-518-6

Typeset by Carnegie Book Production, Lancaster
Printed and bound in Poland by BooksFactory.co.uk

The manufacturer's authorised representative in the EU for product safety is: Easy Access System Europe, Mustamäe tee 50, 10621 Tallinn, Estonia https://easproject.com (gpsr.requests@easproject.com)

PREFACE

I shall not repeat the adage that one should never judge a book by its cover: the quality of volumes in the *Translated Texts for Historians* series is determined by their contents. Even so, and from a very early stage in its history, the series has had a distinctive visual brand. In her reflections on *TTH*'s twentieth anniversary, Gillian Clark noted the series' association with its "candy-coloured covers",[1] a feature amply demonstrated by the striking appearance of the series on Liverpool University Press stands at conferences.

From early in the series' history, *TTH* covers were also characterised by line drawings of appropriate images. Photographs were occasionally, but sparingly, used. I first drew a cover for Wolf Liebeschuetz's translation of *Ambrose of Milan: Political Letters and Speeches* in 2005, volunteering to do so at a relatively late stage in the volume's production when something was needed in a hurry. By that point, the series was associated with excellent cover drawings by Gail Heather and Roger Tomlin; occasionally other artists known to volume authors were used. But gradually since then, drawing the cover images has fallen to me, alongside those for the supplementary series *Translated Texts for Historians, Contexts*, as well as for several volumes (until 2024) of *Translated Texts for Byzantinists*.

Drawing the cover images has always been an interesting project. In most cases the images are proposed by the authors themselves, although occasionally they have asked me to suggest things (and it is very flattering to have these ideas, particularly the unconventional ones, welcomed so enthusiastically). The range of sources has varied considerably: from late antique coins, mosaics, and sculptures to medieval manuscripts and early modern representations of late ancient subjects. Sometimes a touch of imagination has been required, such as the "plastic surgery" to restore the damaged face of the courtier shown on the silver *missorium* receiving codicils from Theodosius I for Scott Bradbury and David Moncur's selection of Libanius' letters (2023). However the image comes my way, in

---

1 G. Clark, "'This strangely neglected author': *Translated Texts for Historians* and Late Antiquity," *Journal of Early Christian Studies* 16 (2008), 131–41, at 133.

every case the simple mechanism of reproducing it by hand in pen and ink encourages in me greater appreciation for the skills and idiosyncrasies of the artists who produced the originals on which the drawings are based. That might be how the sixth-century illuminators of the Rabbula Gospels used the technique, which every child knows instinctively, of using a blue strip at the top of an image to indicate the sky; or how the late-eighth-century mosaicists at Umm-er Rasas, in defiance of their rigidly two-dimensional medium, endeavoured to depict curved bastions flanking the gates of Gaza. And the process encourages me to keep learning, for example about the use of Pahlavi to render the Islamic profession of faith on the coin that graced the cover of Christian Sahner's volume on the *Definitive Zoroastrian Critique of Islam* (2023).

In short, while the focus of *TTH* has always been chiefly, and rightly, on texts, those texts have existed in dialogue with various images. Engaging with those images – and discussing them with volume authors, other editors of the series (particularly Mary Whitby, Gillian Clark, and Phil Booth), and the team at Liverpool University Press (especially Clare Litt, Alison Welsby, and Patrick Brereton) – has ever been an inspiring and humbling privilege. My thanks to all involved.

Mark Humphries
Ynysmeudwy
March 2025

1. Based on an eighteenth-century wall painting in Sadad (Syria), depicting Severos in his patriarchal vestments. Drawing by Mark Humphries. Cover image for *Two Early Lives of Severos, Patriarch of Antioch*, translated with an introduction and notes by Sebastian Brock and Brian Fitzgerald.

2. Gold solidus depicting Aelia Eudoxia Augusta (400–404), wife of the emperor Arcadius. Struck at Constantinople circa 400–401. Drawing by Mark Humphries. Cover image for *The Funerary Speech for John Chrysostom*, translated with an introduction and commentary by Timothy D. Barnes and George Bevan.

3. Bede (or the apostle John) sharpens his pen: Cambridge, St John's College H.6, fol. ii (England circa 1160–1170). Bede's *Commentary on Revelation*, with Caesarius of Arles' commentary and hagiographical and moral treatises. Drawing by Mark Humphries. Cover image for *Bede: Commentary on Revelation*, translated with introduction and notes by Faith Wallis.

4. An Ecumenical Council, drawn by Mark Humphries from an icon (1591) by the Cretan painter Michael Damaskinos, *The First Ecumenical Council*, in St Catherine's church, Herakleion. Cover image for *The Acts of the Second Council of Nicaea (787)*, translated with notes and an introduction by Richard Price; *The Canons of the Quinisext Council (691/2)*, translated with an introduction and notes by Richard Price; and *The Acts of the Council of Constantinople of 869–70*, translated by Richard Price with an introduction and notes by Federico Montinaro.

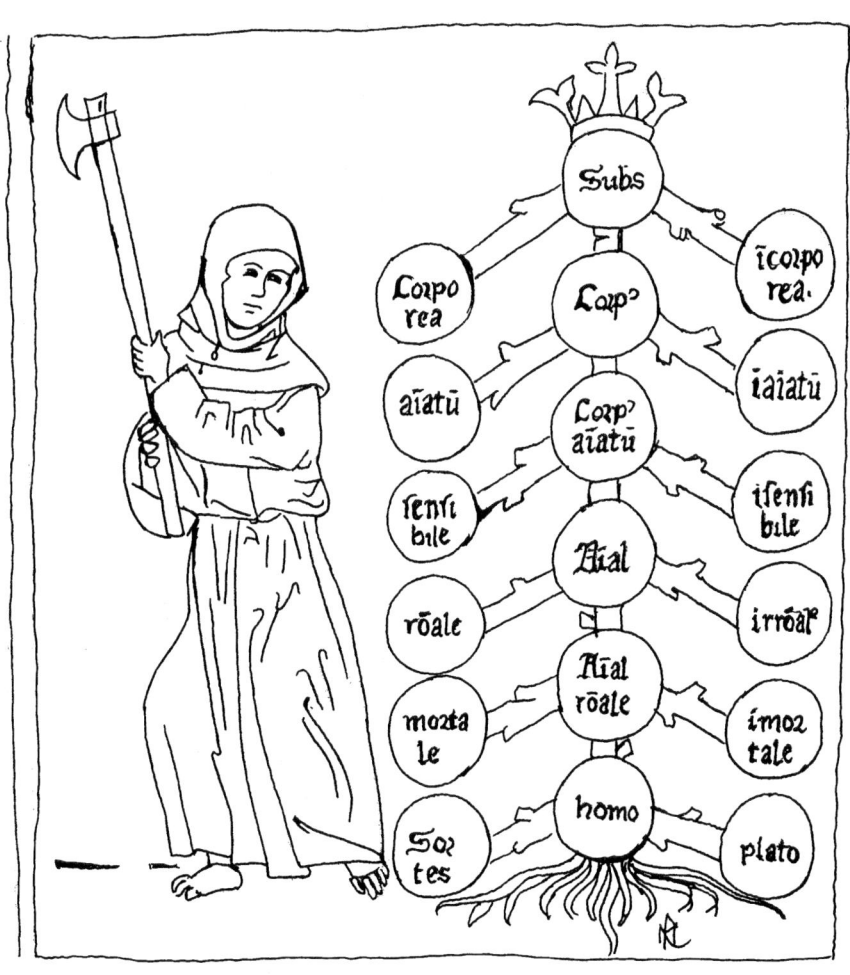

5. "The axe is laid to the root of the tree" (Luke 3:9). The destruction of the tree of philosophical categories, based on an illustration from the *Destructio sive eradicatio totius arboris Porphirii* (Bologna, 1503). Drawing by Mark Humphries. Cover image for *Macarius: Apocriticus*, translated with introduction and commentary by Jeremy M. Schott and Mark J. Edwards.

6. Wall painting from the Umayyad palace of Qasr al-Hayr al-Gharbi, northeast of Damascus, showing mounted archer in Persian style (now kept in National Museum of Damascus). Drawing by Mark Humphries. Cover image for *Khalifa ibn Khayyat's History on the Umayyad Dynasty (660–750)*, translated with introduction and commentary by Carl Wurtzel and prepared for publication by Robert G. Hoyland.

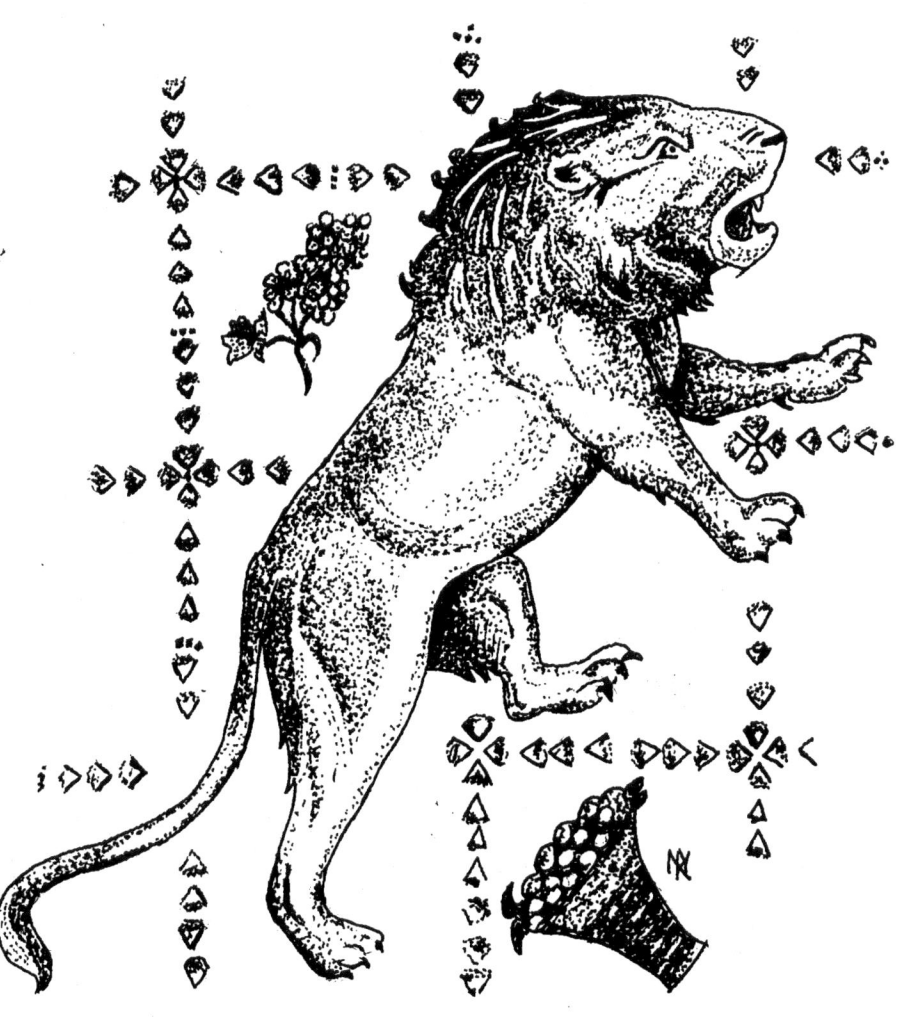

7. Striding lion (early fifth c.) from Antioch floor mosaic. Drawing by Mark Humphries. Cover image for *Between City and School: Selected Orations of Libanius*, translated with introduction and notes by Raffaella Cribiore.

8. Rutilantem, the first word from the preface to Book I of Jonas's *Vita Columbani*, from a tenth-century manuscript produced in Bobbio (Turin, Biblioteca Nazionale, F.IV.12, fol. 5r). Drawing by Mark Humphries. Cover image of *Jonas of Bobbio: Life of Columbanus*, *Life of John of Réomé*, and *Life of Vedast*, translated with introduction and commentary by Alexander O'Hara and Ian Wood.

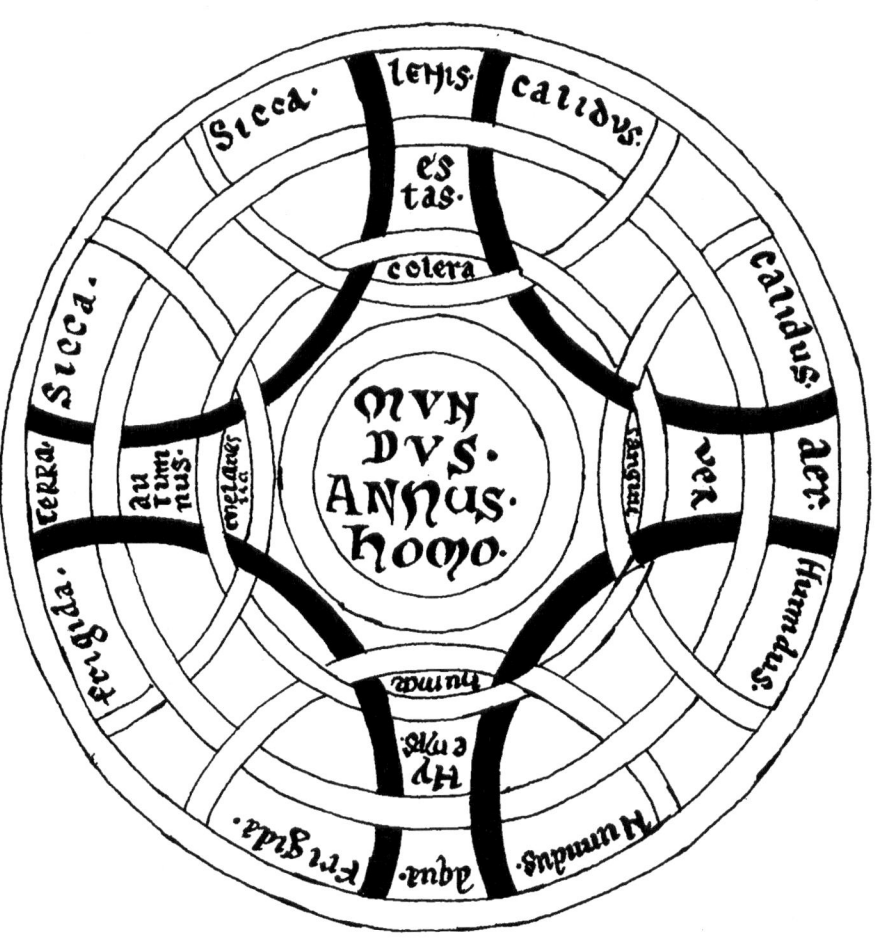

9. MVNDVS – ANNVS – HOMO diagram from a twelfth-century manuscript of Isidore's *De Natura Rerum* (British Library, Harley 3099, fol. 157r.). Drawing by Mark Humphries. Cover image of *Isidore of Seville: On the Nature of Things*, translated with introduction, notes, and commentary by Calvin B. Kendall and Faith Wallis.

10. Geometric wreath mosaic from Carthage, fourth century AD, based on an original now in the National Gallery of Victoria, Melbourne. Drawing by Mark Humphries. Cover image for *The Donatist Schism: Controversy and Contexts*, edited by Richard Miles.

11. Constantius II in consular robes. From the *Chronography of AD 354*, a medieval copy of a fourth-century almanac. Drawing by Mark Humphries. Cover image for *Imperial Invectives Against Constantius II: Athanasius of Alexandria, Hilary of Poitiers and Lucifer of Cagliari*, translated with introduction and commentary by Richard Flower.

12. Detail from the interior of the mezquita of Córdoba. Drawing by Mark Humphries. Cover image for *The Eulogius Corpus*, translated with introduction and notes by Kenneth Baxter Wolf, and *The Indiculus luminosus of Paul Alvarus*, translated with introduction and notes by Kenneth Baxter Wolf.

13. David as Victor, in the 'Durham Cassiodorus' (Durham Cathedral Library MS B.II.30, fol. 172v), a copy of an abridged version of Cassiodorus's *Commentary on the Psalms* written in Northumbria between 725 and 750. Drawing by Mark Humphries. Cover image for *Bede: On First Samuel*, translated with introduction and commentary by Scott DeGregorio and Rosalind Love.

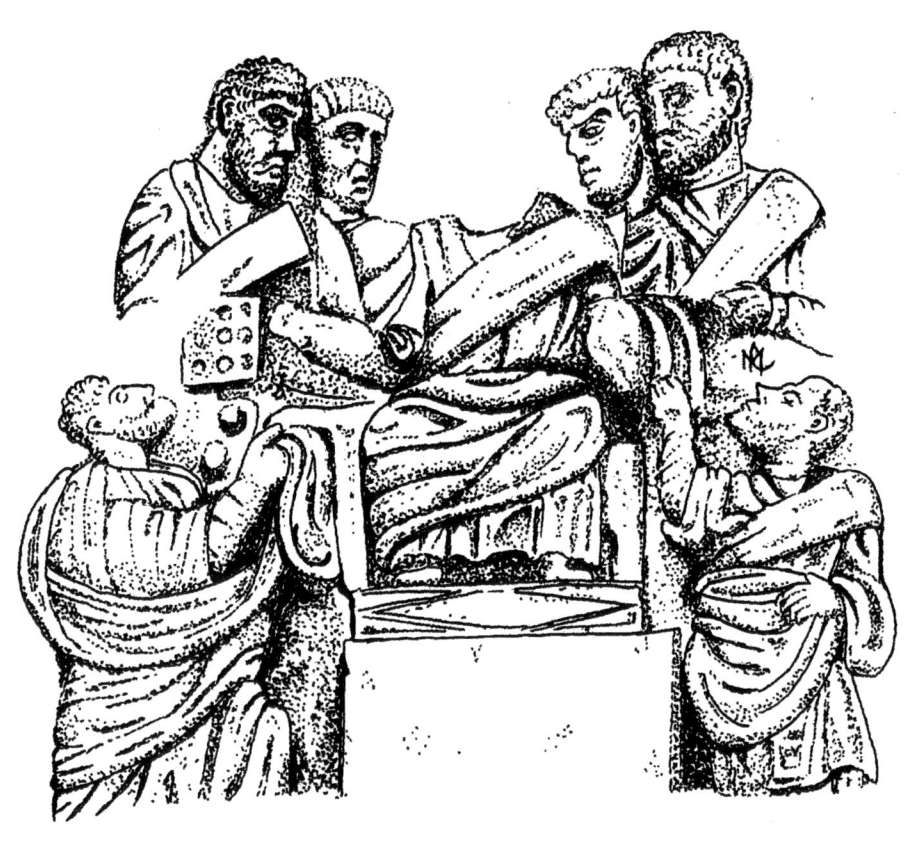

14. Detail from the Arch of Constantine, Rome. Drawing by Mark Humphries. Cover image for *Imperial Panegyric from Diocletian to Honorius*, edited by Adrastos Omissi and Alan J. Ross.

15. Arator presents his work to the abbot Florianus. Based on a twelfth-century manuscript in the Herzog August Bibliothek, Wolfenbüttel. Drawing by Mark Humphries. Cover image for Arator: *Historia Apostolica*, translated with introduction and notes by Richard Hillier.

16. The Council of Ephesus, based on a fresco of 1513 by Simeon Axenti from the church of St Sozomenos, Galata, Cyprus. Drawing by Mark Humphries. Cover image for *The Council of Ephesus of 431: Documents and Proceedings*, translated by Richard Price with an introduction and notes by Thomas Graumann.

17. Woodcut by Hans Burghmair of Alboin, king of the Lombards, and Athanaric, king of the Goths, from the title page of Jordanes, *De Rebus Gothorum*, and Paul the Deacon, *De Gestis Langobardorum*, Augsburg: Johannes Miller, 1515. Drawing by Mark Humphries. Cover image for *Jordanes: Romana and Getica*, translated with introduction and notes by Peter Van Nuffelen and Lieve Van Hoof.

18. Gold multiple of Valens, minted 375–378, set in a medallion, now in the Kunsthistorisches Museum, Vienna. Drawing by Mark Humphries. Cover image for *Themistius and Valens: Orations 6–13*, translated, annotated, and introduced by Simon Swain.

19. Gold solidus of Anthemius, minted at Rome. Obverse: portrait of Anthemius in military dress. Reverse: Anthemius and Leo I stand side by side under a legend proclaiming *Salus Reipublicae* (Safety of the State). Drawing by Mark Humphries. Cover image for *Sidonius Apollinaris: Complete Poems*, translated with introduction and commentary by Roger Green.

20. Scenes of the Crucifixion and Resurrection, based on a painted miniature bound with the sixth-century Rabbula Gospels. Drawing by Mark Humphries. Cover image for *The Festal Letters of Athanasius of Alexandria, with the Festal Index and the Historia Acephala*, translated with commentary by David Brakke and David M. Gwynn.

21. The emperor Theodosius I presents a civilian official with a diptych containing his duties and insignia of office. Reconstructed from the Missorium of Theodosius. Drawing by Mark Humphries. Cover image for *The Letters of Libanius from the Age of Theodosius*, translated with commentary by Scott Bradbury and David Moncur.

22. Coin ascribed to ʿAbd al-ʿAzīz ibn ʿAbdallāh ibn ʿĀmir, Zubayrid governor of Sijistān, 72 AH/691–92 AD (actually minted by Abū Bardhāʿa, Umayyad governor Sijistān, ca. 79–81 AH/698–701 AD?). Obverse: Portrait of a Sasanian king. Reverse: Islamic profession of faith in Pahlavi: "There is one God, there is no other god, Muḥammad is the prophet of God" (yazd-ēw bē ōy anīy yazd nēst mahmat paygāmbar ī yazd). Drawing by Mark Humphries. Cover image for *The Definitive Zoroastrian Critique of Islam: Chapters 11–12 of the Škand Gumānīg-Wizār by Mardānfarrox son of Ohrmazddād*, translated with commentary by Christian C. Sahner.

23. The evangelist Luke from the Lindisfarne Gospels. Drawing by Mark Humphries. Cover image for *Bede: Commentary on the Gospel of Luke*, translated with introduction and notes by Calvin B. Kendall and Faith Wallis.

24. Mosaic of the Virgin Mary from the apse of Cefalù cathedral, Sicily. Drawing by Mark Humphries. Cover image for *Theodore Syncellus: The Homilies 'On the Robe' and 'On the Siege'*, translated with introduction and notes by Michael Whitby.

25. Detail of an ivory relief of the archangel Michael, mid-sixth century, Constantinople. Based on an original in the British Museum. Drawing by Mark Humphries. Cover image for *Theodore of Sykeon: The Life by George and the Encomium by Nicephorus*, translated with introduction and notes by Michael Whitby with Richard Price.

26. Gaza depicted in the eighth-century mosaic pavement from the church of St Stephen at Umm er-Rasas, Jordan. Drawing by Mark Humphries. Cover image for *Mark the Deacon: Life of Porphyry of Gaza*, translated with introduction and notes by Jeff Childers, Claudia Rapp, and Michael Whitby.

27. Augustine debates with the Donatists, based on a painting of 1753 by Charles-André van Loo (1705–1765) in Notre-Dame des Victoires, Paris. Drawing by Mark Humphries. Cover image for *The Conference of Carthage in 411*, translated with introduction and notes by Erika Hermanowicz and Neil McLynn.

28. The Council of Nicaea, with Constantine presiding and the writings of heretics condemned to the flames, based on a drawing from an early-ninth-century canon law compendium in Vercelli (Biblioteca capitolare MS CLXV). Drawing by Mark Humphries. Cover image for *Documents of the Early 'Arian' Controversy and the Council of Nicaea*, translated with an introduction and notes by David M. Gwynn, Richard Price, Michael Whitby, and Philip Michael Forness.